A RECTOR'S DAUGHTER IN VICTORIAN ENGLAND

Published by

Volunteers of America

3939 North Causeway Boulevard
Metairie, Louisiana 70002

©1994 by Volunteers of America, Inc.
Printed in the United States
First Edition

Library of Congress Catalog Card Number: 94-062-068
ISBN: 1-885-287-01-1

A RECTOR'S DAUGHTER IN VICTORIAN ENGLAND

Memories of Childhood And Girlhood

by Maud Ballington Booth

with a forward and epilogue by Susan F. Welty

illustrated by Madeleine Faust

*Saint Anne's Church
Limehouse, London*

Contents

Forward vi
I. My Little Eden 1
II. Behind Rectory Gates: in Limehouse 14
III. Ventures in a Wider World 31
IV. The Rectory Ghost 47
V. We Go Away to School—and Florrie Grows Up 54
VI. I Grow Up, Too 71
VII. Difficult Engagement, Happy Ending 84
Epilogue 101

WHY SHOULD THIS bit of Maud Ballington Booth's autobiography be worth publishing, decades after her death, when the national admiration she earned while she lived has been almost forgotten?

The best reason is that it is a good story, virtually unknown. It is good in two ways; it is both interesting and encouraging.

The contrast between Maud Charlesworth's restricted, upper-class upbringing a hundred years ago and the career she developed is fascinating. The stratified, class-conscious, religiously rigid society in which she grew up differed sentimentally and technologically from that in the late Twentieth Century, but the human problems, in different dress, are much the same: to establish one's own identity, to learn how to live a good life in a family, and to discover how to bridge the gap between the rich and the poor in society. Some of Maud's attempted solutions were funny, but anyone laughing at them is gaining at the same time a better understanding of his forebears and more sympathy for his own generation and its puzzle to find better solutions.

Present day women, caught in the struggle for more rights and recognition, can take courage from this story of a prototype who overcame restrictions worse than theirs. In each of the organizations in which she spent her career, the Salvation Army and the Volunteers of America, she was in part the cause and in part the product of arrangements in which, far ahead of the customs of the time when these organizations were founded, women were rated as equals with men and distinguished themselves as much.

Mrs. Booth would not allow her biography to be written while she lived. Her notebooks, entitled "Memories," were begun in 1931 and soon laid aside. They were found after her death and given to me by Mrs. Booth's daughter Theodora. I referred to them in *Look Up and Hope*, my biography of Mrs. Booth written in 1961. After thirty-three years, "Memories" have been rediscovered.

— Susan F. Welty
Beloit, Wisconsin
August 1994

Susan F. Welty, editor of these memoirs, is also the author of Look Up and Hope, *a biography of Mrs. Booth which was written in 1961 and published by Thomas Nelson & Sons, New York.*

Chapter 1

MY LITTLE EDEN

HAPPY IS THE child born in the country, away from ugly streets and city noise and dirt. I came into the world in the peaceful, beautiful, little village of Limpsfield, Surrey, on September 13, 1865.

Limpsfield had only one long village street of thatched cottages, with here and there a fine house on extensive grounds. The Inn and the blacksmith's shop marked where the wide sweep of the common, covered with honey-sweet, yellow gorse bushes, began. Off in many directions went shady lanes lined with hawthorn bushes and wild roses in their seasons, and masses of primroses and deep purple violets in spring.

My father Samuel Charlesworth was the Rector of St. Peter's Church, which stood just across the street from the Rectory where our family lived. The church was small and very old; some of its stones were thought to date back to an original building in the ninth century. The church records went back to the first Rector in the days of Queen Elizabeth. There was a lych gate through which funerals always passed on the way to the tree-shaded graveyard.

I was only four years old when my father moved to a London parish, but I have some vivid memories of Limpsfield and our lives there. One of the earliest of these recollections is of myself standing with my sister Florrie, her arm around me, as we watched a solemn, little procession pass through the lych gate, to be met by our father in his white surplice. The funeral was for my Grandfather Charlesworth.

I remember, too, the fox hunts that used to sweep over the fields with the red-coated huntsmen racing on their galloping horses after the baying hounds. One day, Florrie and I stood in the Rectory garden watching them riding toward us across our own fields beyond the hedge. A quivering red form flashed by us and dashed for safety into an outhouse we called the "knife-house", because the kitchen boy cleaned the knives there. We rushed behind the fox and locked the door. The horsemen, preceded by the hounds, respected the Rectory gardens but questioned us about whether and where we had seen the fox. We both put on the air of stupid infants who knew nothing. The poor, panting, frightened fox, that we passionately wanted to save, lay safely hidden.

Some of the huntsmen dined at our house that night. How we wanted them to go away! A distant cousin, whom I hated because he wanted to kiss us, was among them. I used to crawl under the table to avoid him.

I was too young to know what the hunt meant, but Florrie knew and she did not like it. Everything Florrie knew was passed on vividly to me and at once adopted by my adoring mind. My beloved sister was the center of my world.

The huntsmen finally remounted. The clatter of hooves grew faint down the village street. The hounds had gone with them and peace reigned. Two little figures in white crept down the garden path; hunted in the bushes for the knife-house door key, which they had thrown there; found it and opened the door wide. They waited quietly for a few moments; then a red flash passed them on its way to liberty. My first prisoner was free for another chance in life.

In another picture etched clearly upon my mind, Florrie was again the central figure. We had a sister named Annie who was six years older than I and four years older than Florrie. Annie was a lover of fairy stories and passed them on to Florrie. She did not often play with us, but Florrie, in her playtime with me, visualized the stories for me. She found the little open space where the fairies danced and the stone tables where they dined and the mossy banks where they slept. But she had to ask Annie where they came into our garden. Where was the entrance to Fairyland?

Beside the street, a long stone gutter carried a lively stream of water after a rain into a dark hole. A big stone pipe in the gutter ran beneath the road, and was determined by me and my two sisters to lead down into the wonders of Fairyland.

Once Florrie had made up her mind just where

the door to Fairyland was, she slipped ahead of our nurses one day and tried to explore. She knelt down and put her head in, but her sturdy little shoulders would not follow and she had to give up. The next best thing to visiting Fairyland herself was to have her beloved baby see its glories and report. So she told me what to do, and the next chance we had, we ran ahead of our nurse—I with great eagerness to obey my leader.

I quickly knelt down in my little white dress to start on my quest. I don't remember anything more, but I was told the sequel. Not only my head but my shoulders passed easily into the mysterious darkness, and only my feet in little blue shoes were to be seen when a terror-stricken nurse arrived. She dragged me, dirty and gasping, into the light. Of course, Miss Florrie was considered very naughty to let her poor little sister do such a thing. I doubt not that punishment followed, but we knew that we had not been naughty at all. We had just felt a very proper explorer's urge—the call of that fairy kingdom we failed to find.

Florrie distinguished herself on another occasion by saving my life. I don't remember the experience for I was too young, but my mother told me about it. On the day it happened, there was a village festival, probably a Sunday School picnic. We were dressed in our pretty white dresses with white socks. My dress had blue ribbons on the shoulders and a big blue sash. In those days there was no bathroom in the big old house, but each room had a bath, prepared by the maids overnight. Florrie and I had our baths in the night nursery. For some reason, the nursemaid had poured water from the hand basins into our bath, making it unusually deep. We had eaten breakfast and were left alone in the nursery until my mother should call for us to go to the picnic.

Nurse and nursemaid had gone down to the kitchen, and we were happy to be by ourselves. We could always think of nice things to do when interfering grownups were not around. Afterward, no one knew, not even I, why I wandered back to the night nursery or how I managed to trip head first into the bath. But Florrie missed her little shadow and ran to investigate. Many five year olds would have screamed and run away, but not Florrie. She screamed, it is true, and she had lusty lungs. But she also pulled and tugged at those blue-shod feet until she had me raised above the water, or I should have drowned ignominiously in little more than my second year. The grownups found a wet, bedraggled, unconscious baby when they rushed in from all corners of the Rectory, and I had no picnic that day.

The Rectory children were taken to church when they were very young, and I was baptized the month after my birth. The services meant little to me, but I remember the setting very well. The Rectory pew was square with high sides; we could not see over them unless we stood on the seats. But high above us, we could see our father in his surplice when he mounted to the pulpit. We could see the high leaded windows with the trees waving beyond them, and sometimes a bird would add a little excitement by flying in around the old beams and rafters. Florrie and I very quietly and surreptitiously built houses with our hymn books for entertainment. A few times, Florrie smuggled in her pet "ladybirds" (or ladybugs, as America knows them) in a little box, and we put them in our "house". Once, Jacker Petterm (why that name, I don't know), Florrie's favorite bug, got away and ran along the edge of the pew. Much scrambling and distress followed until we recaptured him. After that experience, ladybirds were strictly forbidden in church.

There was one interest we were allowed during church services. When the time came for hymns or chants, we were allowed to stand up on the seats.

The fun was to see who could scramble up first. Then we had a full view of the congregation. Florrie was always a sociable little soul, and she would smile and nod at our village friends. I was dreadfully shy. If I caught someone looking at me and smiling, I would shake my curls over my eyes until I could not see. I had the idea that when I lost sight of others I could not be seen.

Florrie was never afraid of anything, but I had two terrors at Limpsfield. One, a dark cupboard, was frightening, but the other was terrifying. It was lions. In the room where I was born and into which Florrie and I sometimes tiptoed when guests did not inhabit it, were two lion heads carved in the posts of the mantlepiece. Our sister Annie told us that at any time they might come to life and roar at us. When I had tight hold of Florrie's hand, I could go in and look at them, but I always had to run when I turned my back to them for fear they had come to life and were following me. When I was alone in that room, I was cold with terror. I don't think that my mother ever knew of my fear. Florrie and I had each other with whom to talk over such mysteries. Since Florrie was my bulwark of protection, I did not feel the need of appealing to grownups for help.

Every Sunday evening of my childhood, we gathered in my father's study, around an open fire in winter, to sing hymns. My father's favorite was "Jerusalem, the Golden," and we always ended with "Abide with me; fast falls the eventide." Heavy curtains shut out the night, and each dear face was clear in the firelight. Florrie and I had little chairs; hers was of cherry wood, mine of mahogany. My sister Annie liked a grownup chair. My mother's lovely face was sweet and smiling, and my father's profile against the fire was calm and serene.

In the study we spoke English, but always in the nursery we spoke French. Although the nursemaid was a village girl, our beloved nurse was French. The thought in those days was that children should learn to speak French while very young, "before their vocal chords were set." When we said our prayers at night and in the morning, we always said them in both English and French. When, in time, a German governess was added to our grownups, we had to say our prayers in German, too. Florrie's and my beds were side by side in the nursery. Annie did not sleep in the "children's" (as she called us) room; she thought herself too grown up.

I remember being taken to a Christmas party at Litsey, Lord Levenson Gower's estate. He was Lord of the manor, the friend of my father's who had given him the living of St. Peter's church parish. I was so shy that being in the festive crowd made me cry to go home. I think that occasion was the first time that Florrie took me in hand and began my Spartan training. She lectured me on courage. She said that to cry was silly and "girlie," and she wanted her little one to be brave. Later on in London days, her training of me became very rigorous. Both of us in later years profited tremendously from the passion for self-control which had taken possession of her active brain.

My lovely, gentle mother did much of our early training, and my father's rules and logic were wise and beneficial, but they were "grown up." I know, as I look back, that my adored Florrie was the real molder of my child-character. My faith in all she said and did was absolute.

Naturally, she often led me into mischief. My faith in her also made me do many erratic things, utterly beyond the comprehension of the adults in the family. But there were always reasons and purposes and imaginings behind these doings which made for a deep interest and constant excitement in life. In our childhood there were no radios, no movies, no phonographs, no theaters, no circuses and few parties. We had few playmates, but we did not want more. We had each other and such wonderful and exciting games that we were busy from morning to night, if only the grownups would not spoil the fun.

Already at Limpsfield, we had our beloved pony Elfie. He was golden brown with a sweeping black tail and mane. My father had a big horse called Taffy, and I loved to be lifted to the saddle when my father came home from his rounds of the parish to ride Taffy with him back to the stable. We had a pony chair which my mother often drove, tucking us children in beside her.

Sights and sounds of Limpsfield have always remained with me. Not far from the Rectory there was a sawmill, and on warm days when the windows were open or we were outside, the buzz of the saw through wood was plain. Rooks nested in the big tree in the church yard, and the "kawr, kawr" of the colony as the birds went to roost at night mingled with my first drowsiness. Climbing up to my mother's window, grew banks of roses and white starred jasmine with lovely fragrance. White snowdrops in their season or Christmas roses in winter grew by the little ferny path to our side gate.

Once my sister Annie's birthday was celebrated with a picnic in the Titsey Woods. I remember

gathering orchids—bee orchids and fly orchids—
and watching hop pickers in the nearby hopfields.
On the hop vines we used to find little caterpillars
which we called "hop dogs" and "hop cats"
because of their funny faces and fuzzy bodies.

All these memories were Limpsfield, small and
rich in woods and fields and flowers. My father
had taken my mother there as a bride. She was his
cousin, Maria Amelia Beddome. Although my
father had come from a long line of clergymen, he
had studied for the bar. With his degree he went
into his Uncle Richard Beddome's law office. My
grandfather was a successful barrister, and my
father, too, was successful in his legal work. But he
was not happy, for he thought the work conflicted
with his Christian principles. So he went again to
college and was ordained, as had been his father
and all his forefathers back to Queen Elizabeth's
time.

Limspfield was his first parish, and he was
greatly loved, but I think my mother was even more
beloved. She had a Bible class for the men of the
village and Mother's Meetings and watched over
the children and visited the cottages. Long, long
after she had been brought back to sleep in that
quiet churchyard, under the carpet of white violets

that grew there, the people would talk lovingly of her with tears in their eyes.

My father was more to the people there than just their spiritual shepherd. He was their friend in time of need. I did not know at the time—perhaps the event occurred before my birth—but when cholera broke out among a gang of road workers on the outskirts of the parish and no one could be persuaded to nurse them, my father went out and was quarantined with them. He was able to save some of them and gave burial to those who died of the dreaded scourge. He was long remembered for that service to his people.

My parents could have stayed all their lives in that lovely village, but when I was not quite four and Florrie was nearing seven, my father felt called to go where he saw the need was greater for Christ's service. My mother sorrowed at leaving Limpsfield and Annie did, also. But my father wanted to work among the London poor, and arranged to exchange parishes with the Rector of St. Anne's in Limehouse. Florrie longed for the excitement of London; and of course, I, her little echo, cheered for London, too. Elfie, our pony, went with us; but Taffy, the horse, disappeared from our lives as did all the country things we knew.

Chapter 2

BEHIND RECTORY GATES: IN LIMEHOUSE

LIMEHOUSE WAS A great East London parish where cargoes of strange things and strange people from over the seas were brought up the Thames River to the east and west London docks. I saw dark-skinned East Indians, slant-eyed Chinese and many other foreigners, to me looking swarthy, queer and wild. Outnumbering them, the poor and ragged of London filled the streets of Limehouse.

Built by a pupil of Christopher Wren, St. Anne's was a big church with a lofty tower. The Rectory dated back to the reign of Queen Anne in the early 1700's. It was a many-gabled house with quite a garden around it and a wide front court. A very high wall surrounded the garden. Great high wooden gates in the wall completely shut off those inside from any sight of busy Commercial Road, the thoroughfare on which they opened. Nothing could shut out the noise and clatter of the street.

Many trees and a big sloping lawn were in our Rectory yard. Mother gave each of us a little space in which to cultivate flowers. She made a rockery for ferns, and flowerbeds filled with color and beauty.

Florrie and I used to save our pennies and buy pansies and pink daisies and lupines for our gardens. Our mother gave us two pennies for every little wheelbarrow filled with dandelions which we weeded out of the lawn. Early on a very hot day, I got my first lesson on thorough weeding. For some reason, I had gone out with Florrie, and I had cut off the dandelions close to the ground. Soon I had my barrow full, but when I took it to my mother to collect my wages, she explained to me that my work had been in vain; every long, hard root had to come out before my load could be accepted.

In new surroundings and in many ways, I was learning more about life. One day, while running up the stairs to find Florrie, a thought suddenly struck me. I stood quite still with the observation.

I said to myself: "Florrie says 'I' and 'me,' too." My reaction may seem stupid to those who have never been suddenly faced with a revelation of identity, but to me the realization came like a thunderbolt. I had always thought of life as surrounding *me*. My mother was there because she was *my* mother, Florrie because she was *my* Florrie.

My home and everything in life I had because they were mine, and if I were not there, they would all vanish. My viewpoint was very egocentric, but it was mine until that moment. I stood and thought it out and realized that Florrie was the center of her life, too, and I one of her surroundings. From that time on, I understood that each individual has his own life, with others around him. Anytime I stand and face a new view of life, I can still see the long staircase and feel the smooth mahogany stair rail under my hand.

To Florrie and me, London was exciting and Limehouse became our beloved home. Studious Annie always disliked it. She was never very strong physically and in a few years was sent away to school. My mother never complained; but she must have found Limehouse with its noise and dust, its poverty and squalor, a difficult contrast to the simple, quiet village and her charming Rectory gardens in Limpsfield. There, too, she had had, in addition to the girls' nurse and nursemaid, a staff including a chambermaid, a waitress, a cook and scullery girl, a houseman, a gardener, an undergardener and a boy in buttons. In Limehouse, aside from a nurse and soon a governess for the girls, only two maids and a boy who took care of the pony and lawn were employed. My mother considered this reduction appropriate, and having a smaller staff never troubled her. But looking back, I can see that she must have had many anxious hours trying to bring up her three little girls in their new home.

First of all, illness was constantly prevalent in the East End of London. We girls caught most of the things going—mumps, measles, whooping cough. At age twelve, I came near death with a ghastly combination of typhoid, pneumonia and smallpox. I was sick for three months and nothing but skin and bone, but my mother's tender nursing pulled me through. Fortunately, perhaps, I was so weak when the smallpox developed that I could not lift my hands to scratch the eruptions, and no scars were left on my face.

But our mother had worse problems than disease to face. We had to be closely watched and guarded from the possible dangers of the neighborhood, of which we children knew nothing. In all those years of London life, we never went beyond the Rectory gates unattended. If we were not with our parents, we had with us a governess or French maid after we had outgrown nurses.

French was still our language, always spoken between us except with our parents. If that had not been so, my mother would have had more fear of the Cockney accent which naturally was all around our neighborhood, so nearly within the sound of Bow Bells. My mother and father spoke the purest English of the cultivated class. Though Florrie and I heard and made fun of the East London vernacular, neither of us ever had trouble with our "H's." We did love to pick up slang, and my mother was constantly telling us that the use of slang was a sign of "poverty of language." She said that if we had a wide and good vocabulary, we would not need slang to express our feelings. We rebelled indignantly against this instruction, but looking back I am thankful for my mother's care. It doubtless helped me as a public speaker.

In Limehouse there soon came into our lives the knowledge of poverty and suffering. My father was a real shepherd to his flock and visited not only his own parishioners but all the lost black sheep of the neighborhood. My mother built a mission house and constantly had Mother's Meetings there; she, also, had men's classes and kindly social events for the poor. She started what was known as a "ragged school." This was a school for the poorest little ones who could not go to the parish school, but who came literally in rags and tatters and barefooted to her classes. They were dirty little mites: underfed, unloved and forlorn. I can remember them grouped around her, especially one poor, cold, battered little fellow standing close to her knee, stroking the fur on her coat with his dirty little hand.

If in those days I had been questioned about religion, I should have thought of our family prayers or our morning Bible class with Mother or our Sunday services at St. Anne's Church. Not realizing it was religion, however, I was slowly absorbing the vision of my parent's ministering lives and my mother's influence on all who knew her. She was beautiful, with a smile that had the light of love and unselfish devotion to God's service behind it. In the sixteen years that I had her, I never saw one thoughtless, selfish, or unkind act; never heard a harsh or unkind word from her lips. And I was proud of her. She often spoke to women's Bible classes in many parts of London, and her clear voice could reach as many as a thousand people.

For many years, she was vice-president of the Mildmay Association. Great churchmen like Bishop Wilberforce took an interest in her work. On one of Bishop Wilberforce's visits to our home, he gave a temperance talk in the parish, and Florrie and I both signed the pledge. I think I was eight and she was eleven.

But to deduce from our parents' earnest lives at the Rectory that we grew up saintly little children would be absurd. We were often imps of mischief. Though Florrie was a peacemaker and thoroughly to be trusted when put on her honor, I was violent-tempered and, often, a really naughty child. My quarrels were mostly with my eldest sister and with my governesses and never with Florrie. I was quick to anger and then utterly uncontrollable. I caused my mother many tears and hours of anxiety, but our mischief was never meant to be unkind or done for wanton caprice. It always had some reason behind it which, alas! was quite obscure to adult eyes.

We had none of the hundred-and-one toys and games invented for children today. We invented our own games and were constantly drawing on very vivid imaginations for amusement.

One of our bloodcurdling games was called

"dried bones," an idea of Florrie's for making a Spartan of her little sister. She had from babyhood wanted to be a boy, and she despised girlish games and actions. She had drummed into my ears, ever since they could convey a thought to my brain, that it was babyish or girlish to cry when you were hurt, or fell, or cut yourself. If I did this unforgivable thing, she was mortified, and I in consequence was overcome with shame.

When she began to study Greek history, she learned of Spartans and their spirit, and she determined to make a Spartan out of her little one. The game was this: we collected hard cushions and hard rubber balls and other missiles. We moved all of the nursery or schoolroom furniture to one side, so as to have a clear battlefield. Then we divided our ammunition, stood in opposite corners of the room and pelted each other fast and furiously, often knocking each other down with our well-aimed weapons. Of course, this could only be done in the hours when we knew that all adults were safely out of the way.

We were often black and blue with bruises, or cut and really sore. But the point of the game was that we must never cry or shed a tear. We must give no sign of hurt. Often my mother would look at us afterward and say, "What have you been doing? I'm afraid my little girls are very rough." But she never learned the reason or method of our Spartan training.

The name for our game came from my father's reading aloud one Sunday the Biblical passage from the Book of Ezekiel about the dry bones in the valley. The next day in our battle, we simultaneously knocked each other down and lay on the floor suppressing all sign or sound of the pain consequent on the furious attack. Florrie's imagination saw the Valley of Dry Bones, and she exclaimed, "Let the dry bones arise!" The name stuck to the game.

In after years if an accident occurred or one of us was painfully hurt, the other would say, "You are a dry bones!" All through our lives, we both bore pain quietly and calmly. I really believe that the silly, childish game developed in us a deep, almost instinctive, self-control.

When dolls were presented to Florrie and me by our mother's friends, we accepted them politely, but we never played with them unless we were alone. On glorious occasions when all grown people were out of the way, we enacted such historic scenes as the executions of Mary, Queen of Scots and Lady Jane Gray, or Joan of Arc being burned at the stake. The dolls figured usefully as leading ladies and were afterwards buried with book and surplice and ringing of bells. One of my wildest fights with my eldest sister came after I had stolen one of her treasured dolls and condemned it to the axe on our "Tower Hill."

Another game ended disastrously for me. It, too, had an underlying reason. The poverty of the people we saw on the streets and in the poor homes where we sometimes went with our mother made a deep impression on us. Florrie began to ask herself, "Why are some people so poor?"

We went shopping with our mother to the linen draper's store (a dry goods store in America), and there we saw flannels and serges and velvets and all sorts of goods. My sister decided that the shopkeepers were cruel to the people and would not sell the goods cheaply enough.

So began our crusade against the storekeepers. Florrie argued that when poor people asked the price of goods, the store people, who had marked their little price tickets far too high, quoted the figure and the poor turned away discouraged. If we could remove those tickets, the sales people would forget the extravagant price and tell the poor the real, lower price, and they could buy the goods.

So we were to go shopping with mother at every chance; and while she was busy, we were to wander around and deftly pull out the pins and remove and pocket the little price tickets. We did this for a few months. We had a big box in which we kept our spoils. When I was out without Florrie, my great pride was to bring back a goodly number.

I was alone with my mother when disaster overtook me. I can still see the ghastly scene. I had slipped the price ticket from a roll of flannel lying on the counter not far from my mother. As ill luck would have it, she saw the flannel and quite unexpectedly asked the price. The girl turned it over, hunted for the ticket, and said, "Strange. I saw it marked a minute ago."

My mother turned to me and asked if I had touched it. In our home lying was an unpardonable sin, and besides, Florrie's childish code of ethics absolutely forbade it. She had instructed me, "Hold your tongue; change the subject if you can. But when you can't, speak the truth. Don't lie!"

So I answered, with burning cheeks, "Yes!"

"That was very mischievous," my mother said. "You must return it at once."

I put my hand in my pocket and pulled out the wrong ticket. I had already worked swiftly and well that day. The second ticket mystified my mother, and she asked if I had more. Just then the lunch bell rang and a number of salespeople filed by, among them the manager. He watched while the Rector's little daughter emptied out a pocket full of tickets. Some onlookers giggled, but my poor mother was distressed. I blushed and blushed and burned with shame and suppressed tears. My mother could get no word from me as to why I had done such a thing, and she and the store people never learned. I was put to bed as soon as we got home, and I suffered my martyrdom indignantly, but all was worth while when Florrie crept into my darkened room and whispered, "Never mind, darling. You're a brick!" Her approval was a high reward.

Most of our days were far from exciting. Hours that seemed very long were spent in the schoolroom with our governess. Sometimes we had a governess who lived with our family; sometimes we had one who came in by the day. Florrie and I thought up endless tricks to play on them and used to boast to each other in private that none ever stayed more than three months. I for one was not very fond of lessons. I loved history and geography and found them easy to remember, but I was a hopelessly bad speller, slow in reading and an absolute blank where arithmetic was concerned. It was a joy when a pea-soup fog blanketed London thickly enough to keep the governess away.

When we had time to ourselves on pleasant days, we could take turns riding Elfie around and around the graveled courtyard. We could be knights on a Crusade or rescuing a damsel in peril, or explorers, or even kings. But ours was a very small kingdom.

To make up a little for that, we were allowed to keep pets. I loved my birds, and so did Florrie, but we had to attend to them ourselves. When there were thirty or more of them, the cleaning of cages and arranging of baths and covering them at night from the cold meant lots of time and trouble.

We had two very privileged characters who lived in the dining room window and were always allowed to come out and hop about the breakfast table. They were Joey, a long-tailed parakeet, gray with yellow crest and pink cheeks, and Bully, a very tame little bullfinch. Their close association made Joey ashamed of his shrill squawks and calls, and he learned the bullfinch song. He rendered it in a very raucous voice, twisting his head and tail and swaying his body with the bullfinch's mannerisms. When the birds ran about the breakfast table accepting tiny pieces of bacon here and of egg there, they always gravitated to the big silver coffeepot where they could see themselves mirrored. Then they would bow and sing to their shadow counterparts. Bully just whispered and sang, but Joey was amorous. He would put out his little round pink tongue to kiss the coffeepot parakeet, and when he burned himself, he would shake his head vehemently.

Once I kept chickens, with a run just off the stableyard: a black Spanish rooster, named Henry the Eighth, and his six wives. Florrie and I wouldn't eat such pets, and I wouldn't even eat the eggs, so the chickens were hardly profitable and were given up. I kept canaries in the schoolroom, and Florrie had a cage there with a pair of dormice. She often took them to the breakfast table and taught them to sit up on their little haunches and fold their hands while grace was said. Then they could fall to on their crumbs of bread.

Our mother bought a little hedgehog to get rid of the huge cockroaches which came from the East Indian docks and infested our basement kitchen.

Of course, Billy was Florrie's and my pet. One of our favorite tricks was to put him in a cupboard where paper and kindling were kept for lighting the kitchen fires. We had a way of fixing the door so that when he felt energetic and started to chase a cockroach, he could push the door open and follow his prey.

One night every week, Mother had a Bible class and hymn-singing meeting with the old widow women of the parish. They would gather around her at our big kitchen table. We would listen for Billy to wake up and scratch and scurry around in his cupboard. A big fat cockroach would slip through the crack and scuttle across the floor; then with a bang the cupboard door would burst open. With quills up and little paws a-gallop, our hedgehog would launch himself in pursuit. Under the chairs of squealing women, the chase would go merrily forward. I don't think mother ever learned that the episodes were all prearranged.

In our home the Sabbath was very strictly observed and meant little free time for us. My father, through all the years of his life, never travelled on Sunday by train or even in the carriage or on horseback. If he was called to someone sick or was helping with a service in a neighboring parish, he always walked, however many miles it might be. When we were old enough, we children always went to two church services on Sunday and in fine weather to three. If the weather was stormy and we stayed at home on a Sunday afternoon, we were not allowed to play any weekday games or to look at weekday books. We had Sunday picture books, but we soon knew them by heart. My father had a service on Sunday afternoon, my mother a Bible class at her mission house, and the governess and maids always had that time away, so Florrie and I had a bad-weather afternoon to ourselves, and it was saved from boredom by one Sunday toy of real delight.

We owned a very big Noah's Ark which had belonged to my mother and her brothers and sisters in their childhood. They must have been most exceptional little children for the ark was handed down to us in a wonderful condition. We added some extra animals and constructed a gangway for them to descend to dry land after the Flood. We had our Bible picture book to help us set the scene, and forming the long procession of animals two by two from the elephants down to the grasshoppers used to take a long time. We had a number of extra monkeys and little white lambs that we had taken from a toy German farm. The procession led round and round the wooden nursery table to the center where Noah, Mrs. Noah, and their sons and daughters-in-law stood around a well constructed altar, built on our picture book design. Under Noah's wooden arm was stuck a dollhouse knife. When all was ready with every last one of the animals standing at attention, the great moment arrived.

We used to run out to the stairs then and listen to make sure that nobody was coming to spoil the fun. If we were safe, we would hurry back to strike the match that would light the sacrificial flame. When Florrie told me to lay the lamb on the altar, we knew that we had chosen it wisely, for we always sacrificed the little broken-legged lambs who could no longer walk in the procession.

How often, in after life, that scene has come back to me when I have realized how much our childish sacrifices typified the gifts of those who bring to God that which they can well spare and won't especially miss—the broken-legged lambs of their possessions.

Our sacrifices burned quite a blackened hole in the table. Many years afterward, I showed it to my children in Florrie's little study at her family's Hertford Heath home.

Chapter 3

VENTURES IN A WIDER WORLD

MY PARENTS REALIZED that we were much restricted to our home and its grounds and took us on holidays when they could. During the school year, these were usually very brief excursions, but in summer Mother would take us children vacationing farther afield.

Our two favorite visiting places near London were my Grandfather Beddome's home at Clapham and my Aunt Maria Charlesworth's pretty cottage at Nutfield.

We always celebrated Christmas at the Beddome home with a big and enjoyable family gathering. Grandfather Beddome was wealthy and very generous to all his children and grandchildren. He would give each of us one of every coin of the realm during our visit, but my mother always made us put our money in the savings bank. We could only spend our tiny weekly allowance.

Aside from our allowances, we never heard talk of money in our home. We children did not think our family wealthy, but we always had enough for all the requirements in the station of life into which we were born. If we wanted things and my mother could not give them to us, she would merely say that she did not wish us to have them. I am glad now that money played no part in our lives as children, for I see in the lives of so many people constant thought and talk and struggle about money. At least when their parents are in the position to carry the financial burden without troubling the children, giving the little ones a few years of unspoiled freedom is good.

We often visited Aunt Maria Charlesworth's home. She was an authoress very well known in Victorian days because of her books for children. *Ministering Children* was the most popular and had been translated into several languages. She also wrote about English village life, which she knew well. She had a beautiful white dog which I loved dearly, as well as ring doves in a wicker cage and several hives of bees. Like our aunt, her cook-housekeeper was our good friend. She was an apple-faced, good-natured countrywoman, and her spotless kitchen was a place of delight.

Miss Charlesworth had a wonderful speaking voice like my father, her brother, had. They were musical, resonant voices that seemed almost to sing and vibrate through the listener's nerves. She used to read Shakespeare's plays to us, and though I was too young to understand them, I was fascinated by strange words and varied tones.

When Florrie was about nine and I about seven, we made Aunt Maria a very lengthy visit. Her cottage belonged to a friendly neighbor, Arthur Barclay, whose family lived at Nutfield Court. Only the church and a quiet old graveyard lay between the cottage and the Court, and we were soon introduced to the three young Barclay boys, who were about our ages. With our attendant governesses supervising, we played with the boys in field and garden and took walks in the wood. Our energetic cricket games wore much of the grass off of Miss Charlesworth's lawn.

A few miles away was the older Barclay estate at Bury Hill near Dorking, where Arthur Barclay's younger brother Charles and his sister Neville lived. Charles was then about eighteen but not above playing with us children. Neville especially liked Florrie, and several times she and Charles drove us to Bury Hill in a high dog cart. Later we had some happy visits at house parties at Bury Hill. We learned to skate, though not very well, on the lake there. On summer visits I can remember sitting in the twilight of my bedroom window and watching dozens of little rabbits frolicking on the grassy hill behind the house. In the barn baby partridges and pheasants were hatched out under old mother hens to restock the lodge-keeper's cottage located at the gate to the big house. The lane was walled in on both sides by great masses of glorious rhododendrons. One day we had a picnic some miles away over the Barclay hills and woods to a "wishing well," a spring amid ferns and hazel trees. The day was memorable because right nearby we found a bullfinch nest and a dormouse nest. The furry brown mouse with its bushy tail and bright eyes watched us warily as he guarded his cozy little abode. Charles Barclay must have thought the time memorable, too, for he became a good friend of Florrie's.

When we went on summer vacations and my father was able to go with us, we usually went on mountain climbing expeditions to Wales. One of these trips must have been two years after we became acquainted with the Barclays and Florrie was recovering from a bad bout with scarlet fever. Charles Barclay spent a day with the family, and afterward said that he made up his mind then, although Florrie was only eleven, that he had loved her since she was nine and intended to marry her when she grew up. I believe that he never looked at another girl, but did love Florrie steadfastly, though he only corresponded with her on a friendly basis for the next few years.

We had more than one wonderful holiday in North Wales when our father took us climbing the hills and mountains. We always explored without guides, which made us feel more adventurous. But I don't think my father was with us on the trip which might have cut short our childish careers.

Mother had taken rooms in the tiny village of Aber in a house surrounded by wide pastures. Through its garden ran a lovely, singing, trout stream. Very early every morning, Florrie and I started out with a basket apiece to gather mushrooms in the fields. One day we were successful and had nearly filled our baskets. We were happily talking and picking in the middle of a big field when we were startled by a dreadful, bellowing roar. A fierce and raging bull was making straight for us with head down and tail thrashing—every sign of anger that bulls are supposed to manifest. I can still feel the burning pain in my chest and throat produced by that wild run to escape. We just reached the stone wall around the field in time. My knees were scraped and bleeding after Florrie dragged me over, and we lay, gasping, on the other side where we fell in a bed of nettles. The baffled bull tore up the ground and bellowed. As we got up and started home, trembling from our run, scratched and nettle-stung, our childlike, inconsolable concern was that all our lovely, fresh mushrooms had been lost in our rush for safety.

It was at Aber, too, that we got into trouble by riding a pig. We had no pony there and in one of the long lanes, to our joy, we found a strong, fat, white pig. We rode it most successfully until the stupid thing got tired and stubborn and insisted on dashing with us into a barnyard. In its haste to get to its own sty, the pig trampled a chicken to death. That afternoon, while we sat demurely sewing and listening to our mother read to us, an irate, old Welsh woman appeared before her with a dead chicken in her basket and a tale of woe about the naughty little girls who had killed it. We were most indignant, for her own stupid pig did the killing, but our side of the case was not listened to for a moment, and we had to give all our pennies for several weeks to pay for that chicken.

On our journeys from London in summer, we travelled in those old-fashioned railroad carriages with windows and doors at the sides and no corridor or aisle. Six people sat on each side facing each other. There were generally five of us—or six, if we had a maid as well as a governess. Our great hope was to have the whole compartment to ourselves. Then we could move about as we pleased, sing, or talk, and always look out of the window. Otherwise, if five or even six strangers were with us, we must sit still and silent.

Florrie and I hit on a plan to reserve the whole carriage. We had both had whooping cough very badly one winter, and we knew exactly how to repeat those dreadful paroxysms most realistically. We would jump into an empty compartment as soon as the train could be boarded; then, if anyone showed any sign of an intention to enter, we both started the much dreaded cough. That made them quickly change their minds. Our scheme really worked very well.

If my father could not spare the time to go with us on summer holidays, my mother usually took us to lovely seaside or mountain resorts: Lowestoft, Harwich, Hastings and Felixstowe at different times. Usually, we stayed in a rented cottage, but at Felixstowe, on the east coast, we were loaned the Allenby home. Mrs. Allenby was a friend of our mother, and her own family was away. I never met her son Edmund, who became the Viscount Allenby of World War I fame. We had a glorious time sailing in the Allenby's yacht, the Waterwitch, and exploring their wide acres.

One day we rode on an old stage coach, running from Felixstowe to Ipswich, to the famous Whitehorse Inn where Dickens' Mr. Pickwick slept one exciting night. To our joy, Florrie and I had the seat on top next to the driver. Sister Annie, Mother and the maid were inside. The two long seats on the top were filled with passengers. As usual, we were talking in French when Florrie hatched a new game. We changed to English and talked in a pretended undertone about how much fun was our unaccustomed mode of travel. How strange to be without our own carriage and footman. How wonderfully Mother played her part without her staff around her. We talked of imaginary friends, whispering titles. At one place where the coach halted, Annie got out and called to us. "How are you children getting on?"

We answered and then laughed heartily. "Think of our lady-in-waiting calling us 'children.' She certainly acted well."

All the journey we whispered and chattered, apparently sure that we were not overheard, but really chuckling at the interested silence and whispers behind us. The climax utterly mystified my mother. Not only were we lifted down with the greatest of care, but the door was held open for her and she was bowed out with much ceremony. The coach driver's whispered words to the landlord of the Whitehorse brought him bowing and scraping before my mother's and Annie's perplexed faces. We mischievous little imps marched into the Inn with our noses in the air, smiling and nodding like royalty to the onlookers. Not until we were washing our faces and being combed and put to rights for dinner did Mother detect some smugness in the air and asked, "What have you children been up to?" But our faces were blankly innocent as we parried the question.

On a vacation at Lewes, in the Downs at Suffolk, I learned to swim. There was a freshwater, open-air swimming pool where the instructor put a harness around our chests and waists and then held us up by a rope while we lay spider-like on the water. I did not seem to get much help thereby, but one day, running around the slippery stone edge of the pool, I slipped into the deep end and sank. Coming up, I promptly struck out for the side of the pool, swimming easily. Strange to say, in those days comparatively few girls or women swam. Later, Florrie and I took lessons from the Beckwith family who were professionals. The first woman to ever try to swim the English Channel taught me to dive. We girls soon became very good swimmers, so much so that often crowds gathered to watch us when we were in the water at bathing resorts.

Other relatives sometimes visited us at the seaside. Our Grandfather Beddome once joined us at Lowestoft. He and my father were amateur astronomers, and he brought his telescope with him. One day when Florrie and I had returned from swimming, he entertained us by letting us look through his telescope at other bathers in the water. To our astonishment we saw our own bathing suits on two maids who had borrowed them just to try them on. We were most indignant.

That vacation must have been the one when our mother took us to visit two great aunts in Ryde since the Isle of Wight was near. In that small country town, we were allowed to go out for several long walks unescorted, and we could enjoy ourselves without adult oversight. We used to go window-shopping, but that soon palled. We longed to go inside the shops and look at the things we would have liked to buy if we had had the money. Our weekly allowance was so small that it usually disappeared in a day. Besides, we felt that we could not go into the stores at all. They were not like big modern department stores where one can saunter around without making a purchase. In this emergency we struck up a plan that gave us infinite amusement.

We spoke French as if we were French, so our plan worked perfectly. We walked in boldly, and Florrie asked pleasantly in French for certain things she wanted. Then the fun began. The salespeople puzzled and puzzled over what she wanted. I, in very broken English, would try to explain. Sometimes we would be the center of quite a group of people all trying to understand and discussing among themselves what we could mean. I wonder that we were ever able to carry through without smiling. Not only were we amused at our own acting, but the things said to us and among themselves by the shopkeepers were often killingly funny. We never did find what we were supposed to be seeking, but when we got away by ourselves we had hilariously good times laughing over our experiences.

We played one very naughty trick on our dear mother. A candy was available that we liked very much, called "cushions." The pieces were large, thick and square, something like taffy, and flavored with peppermint. Each one was a mouthful. When you bit into one, it almost stuck your jaws together. Several minutes of hard work were needed to get through one. Perhaps our liking them came from their lasting qualities. When we got them, we got our money's worth.

Our mother had seen our joyful mastication of these delights, but had never ventured to try one herself and did not realize their qualities. One bright summer day, we were wandering through the streets of the little seaport town of Seaford, south of Lewes, when we persuaded her to take one.

When mother took us on holidays, she always made a point of getting acquainted with the local Rector. She had become well known to the Rector of the Seaford parish church, for she had helped with his Bible class work, and he esteemed her greatly. His name, which I have reason to remember well, was William Mead Buck.

On the day in question, when my mother had just yielded to our urgent request to slip a big fat sticky "cushion" into her mouth, who should appear advancing toward us but the genial Rector. Poor Mother! She could not speak. She could not swallow the horror in her mouth or hope for quick relief. For the next few minutes, she spent her time dodging down sidestreets and byways with her little imps of children shrieking with laughter.

Several times Dr. Buck happened to call when we children sat hungrily at the dinner table waiting for a delayed mother. One memorable day we were to have duck and green peas, and we were very hungry after our swim. Mother was just going to carve the bird when the maid announced that Mr. Buck was in the drawing room and wished to speak with her. The duck went back to the oven, and we sat at the table getting more and more hungry and aggravated. On the spur of the moment, we composed a verse and consoled ourselves by singing it to a tune of our own, with a knife and fork accompaniment:

Mrs. Buck smelled the duck,
   And she said to William Mead,
"Get your hat and cravat,
   And go see those Charlesworths feed."

Poor Mother, trying to be polite and pleasant in the drawing room, heard her naughty children rolling out a song, the full meaning of which she feared might at any moment penetrate through her flurried conversation and reach William Mead's comprehension. Fortunately, he left, apparently without the worst happening.

Whether we were on vacation or at home, Florrie and I were nearly inseparable. She shared everything with me. Sometimes she wrote stories and read them to me, and I thought them thrilling. They may have foretold her gifts as a writer of fiction, but I soon forgot them. Everything she did I admired and tried to imitate, though I could never sing and help in our parent's meetings as she could. She had wonderful brown eyes, and I thought her the most beautiful person on earth.

I was very sensitive about my own appearance. Looking long and sorrowfully into the mirror convinced me that I was ugly. I disliked turned up noses because I wanted a straight one like Florrie's, but I became obsessed with the idea that my nose was of the wrong variety, especially after I fell off of a tall chair and knocked my nose upward. If my sisters wanted to tease me, they called me "Turn-Up." I flew into many a childish rage at this insult and shed bitter tears over my affliction. Florrie eventually assured me that although my nose was not shaped like hers, it really never was "retroussé." But I was seventeen before the knowledge that any one could attribute good looks to my face dawned upon me; I came too far short, in my opinion, from Florrie's beauty.

Nothing, though, detracted from the strong bond of love and loyalty between Florrie and me. All through life, we seemed to have almost a telepathic way of communicating silently when others were in the room with us. Even when the Atlantic Ocean separated us and we were apart for long years, this thought transference worked. She would write me a little note asking me some question or speaking of some subject on her mind, and the same day I would write to her and answer her questions, so that the letters crossed each other.

In my closely guarded and sheltered life in Limehouse, I had no touch of sorrow or tragedy in my early years, and the only temptations I had to fight were those from within, created by a quick temper, a love of fun rather than duty, and a natural inclination to shirk things I did not like. I resented the restrictions and order of my elders. All children with spirit must be trained and guided, and I suppose all of them, like young colts, resist the bit and rein.

As I look back, how thankful I am that I was born in a home where I was taught restraint and law and order and self control. Surely such a home is the small beginning for the wider world where God's law and order and the rights of others must be respected and obeyed if we would live life safely, sanely and happily and be of some use and blessing to others.

My sisters and I were well grounded in Bible study, for that was our mother's daily part of our education. I was teaching a Sunday School class when I was thirteen. I believe that Florrie from early childhood was an earnest, understanding Christian, but I was only a formal one. Of course, I prayed. I went to church. I believed in the truths my parents taught me, but I had no vital personal faith and experience until I was sixteen.

Chapter 4

THE RECTORY GHOST

MOST CHILDREN ENJOY shivering over ghost stories, knowing that they are only stories. Our Charlesworth family lived for twelve years in the Limehouse Rectory with a real ghostly mystery. The feeling we developed was certainly never terror but, at first, some nervousness. In time that became merely a questioning interest and a thrill in the manifestation of something that we never understood.

I am not a believer in spiritualism. I do not want to go on record as a believer in the return of departed spirits. I think if spirits were permitted to return, they would come for some good and helpful reason. But there was something very strange and utterly unexplainable in our home, a fact that every member of our family could attest to.

We always talked of the manifestation as "the ghost." We spoke in as matter of fact way about its footsteps as if we had asked, "Did you hear the cat run up the stairs last night?" At times the ghost was very active; then for days or even weeks we heard nothing. At first when we heard the strange sounds like footsteps, my parents thought that one of the servants must be a sleep-walker or that rats were in the house. But all such theories failed to account for the phenomenon.

Every evening we had family prayers, led by my father. I can well remember times when all the servants were kneeling with us and my father's voice was lifted in divine worship; that we would hear hurried footsteps run up from the basement kitchen, pass along the hall and rush up the long flight of stairs to the next floor, across the upper hall, and, then, actually race up the flight above. They were such real and solid steps that after prayers were over, we would go and hunt through the rooms above. The funny part of the matter was that the steps would go up, and then stop, not returning. Yet, at other times, they would start above and come down.

Once when my mother had taken us children away for the summer, my father was alone in the house except for the cook and housemaid, who slept at the top of the house. They had gone to their rooms and my father had locked his door and was enjoying a hot bath. Suddenly, he heard footsteps come down the stairs and stop at his door. He shouted, "Who is there?" There was no answer, but he saw the handle of the door turn and then the door was shaken. He heard no more footsteps, so he jumped up from his bath, threw something around him and opened the door, but no one was there.

Next morning he asked the women if they had gone down after once retiring. The carpets had been taken up from the stairs and that made the footfalls especially clear. Both cook and housekeeper denied having done so, but the cook remarked with some indignation that she had heard him come up and go into Miss Annie's room next to hers. She had remarked to the maid that she wondered what the master could be doing there so late at night.

Certain boards on the stairs and in the passages creaked, as they often do in old houses, and we could follow the progress of the ghost as he passed over them. In the passage outside the schoolroom door, a gymnastic swing with stirrups was hooked over a nail when not in use. The ghost loved to jingle the stirrups in passing. My father's room was opposite the schoolroom, and late one night, he heard the stirrups jingle, the schoolroom door banged open and the sound of drawers being yanked open and slammed shut. So noisy was the ghost that night that Father was sure we children had been in the room on some prank of our own. He asked us at breakfast what on earth we had been doing. We told him, truthfully, that we knew nothing about the noise. He went with us to the room, and we found all our books and pens and pencils thrown around the room in disorder. Naturally, we came to the opinion that someone in the house must be to blame, but no one could ever be caught. When old servants left and new ones came who knew nothing of the ghost, they too heard and talked about the mysterious noise.

When I was nearly at death's door with typhoid fever, my mother was watching beside my bed. She heard the footsteps come down the stairs. They crossed the passage making straight for my room. My mother sprung up and locked the door; she stood back watching and listening. The steps came close and she saw the door handle quietly turning. Then it stopped. The footsteps retreated across the passage and down the stairs. My mother was not an excitable or nervous person, but she felt that the locking of the door was absolutely necessary to protect me from danger. No one could explain the occurrence.

In the 1870's and 1880's, much was written about "odic force." This power was described as a strange influence that some people unconsciously exerted over inanimate objects, causing furniture to move and making strange knockings. But that could not explain our ghost, as the footsteps had nothing to do with the presence or absence of any member of the family. Of that we were convinced by the experience of years.

The last strange happening and the only time anything queer was seen occurred just before my father left St. Anne's parish and its Rectory. My sister Florrie had married; my mother had died, and I was away at school. He was living alone with my sister Annie and the servants.

Returning from a parochial call and approaching the Rectory, he saw a group of people in Commercial Road, gazing over the high wall at the Rectory roof with its many gables and chimneys. He heard some one say, "There he goes now, behind that chimney!"

Then someone recognized my father and said, "Here is the Rector."

Father asked what they were looking at, and they told him, "The man on the Rectory roof." He saw no one, but they told him that the man had just passed behind a chimney and that he had been dressed like a parson but looked queer. Pressed, they could not explain the queerness except that he wore a long black coat like a cleric's, but it looked old fashioned.

Hurrying to the house, father ran upstairs to my sister Annie's room, the only one with a small balcony. The window was open. By putting a ladder on that balcony, some one might have climbed to the roof, but there was no sign of a ladder or rope. Father went back down to the garden and looked at the roof from all sides, but no prowling figure was disclosed.

We never solved the mystery of the ghost. My father learned that at the time the plague devastated London in 1664 and 1665, the then Rector of Limehouse deserted his parish and fled to the country instead of standing by the dying and burying the dead. The dread scourge he fled from pursued him, and he died in the country. My father said if the unhappy souls of those who were faithless to their trust were made to haunt the scene of their cowardice, the long ago shepherd of the smitten flock might be our restless ghost.

My sister Florrie, who years afterward became a member of the Society for Psychical Research, had another theory. She thought that many of the sounds in the old house might be echoes of impressions left long ago by someone who went through an agonizing experience. That would not have been the faithless shepherd, because our Rectory had been built since his time. But inanimate objects might have received the impression from some disturbed soul just as a photographic plate receives an image. Then certain people attuned to receive the impression might hear the sound or even see a scene repeated years afterward. Florrie, in fact, long afterward wrote her novel *The Upas Tree* in which a critical incident is based on this idea.

Personally, I have no theory. I only know what we heard, and the real interest and excitement these experiences provided our home life.

Chapter 5

WE GO AWAY TO SCHOOL—AND FLORRIE GROWS UP

EARLY ONE YEAR our parents decided that Florrie and I were to go to school in Switzerland. My mother planned to take us and stay nearby until we were settled and happy in the new environment. My sister Annie was already in a finishing school in Lausanne, but we were entered in a French school in Grassiere. We had not been there long when typhoid broke out, and three of the older girls died. My mother moved us to Mrs. Hooper's school at Vevey. We had only been there a short time when Florrie showed signs of fever. Mother had to take a cottage belonging to one of the hotels and start a siege of nursing. I was left at school, homesick and forlorn, and earned a reputation for laziness where lessons were concerned. My only joy was when school walks took us past the cottage where my beloved Florrie was shut in, and I could see my mother's face at the window.

When school closed and Annie joined us from Lausanne, Florrie was well again. We all went to the mountains for a glorious summer amid flowers and waterfalls, forests and glaciers, all painted in my memory in beautiful, vivid colors. We waded in ice cold streams fed from the glaciers high above us and picnicked in dark pine forests. We climbed to dizzy heights to gather edelweiss and rested while mother read to us in Alpine pastures, blue with gentians. In the evening we watched the snowy peaks flush to crimson, pink and orange, or glitter white and ghostly under the moon's bright light. Then we all went home to Limehouse, but Annie soon left to attend Hill House, Belstead, a girls' school in Suffolk, which our mother had attended years before. The headmistress, Mrs. Umphelby, was her close friend and my second Godmother.

While we lived in Limehouse, Florrie and I had no playmates or intimate friends in our neighborhood. When I was about thirteen, our family became good friends of Dr. and Mrs. Grattan Guinness and their family, who lived at Harley

House in the Bow Road about half an hour's walk from our Rectory. Geraldine was Florrie's age and her chum; Lucy was my age and mine. There were three younger children at home, too; a boy and two small sisters. Harry, the older son, was away at school.

Our parents arranged for Geraldine and Lucy to come to the Rectory and share our governess. We all enjoyed the arrangement. On half-holidays we could go to Harley House and play. But the next year, Florrie was sent to Belstead. I missed her terribly and hated lessons. Geraldine did not come for them any longer, but Lucy was still my chum and my only young companion.

One of my first realizations of tragedy came when diphtheria attacked the Guinness family. Mrs. Guinness, Geraldine, little Phoebe and the baby daughter were stricken. Lucy came to live with my family in those dreadful days, and my mother was the one who had to tell her that both her little sisters had died.

The next year, I, too, was sent to Belstead, but Lucy and I remained friends for many years, until the Guinness family scattered to foreign mission fields.

Even in her early teens, Florrie had been a great help to our parents in parish meetings, singing and leading music. My mother regretted parting with her, but did so for a reason. Since their meetings in her childhood, Charles Barclay had travelled around the world, studied for the church and been ordained; he had persuaded my father to take him as his curate. But when he asked to court Florrie, my father made him promise not to say anything to her about marriage until she was eighteen. Belstead was a good place for her to be.

Her second and last year was my first. Annie had already gone to attend Girton, the first women's college in England, established in 1866. To have Florrie with me to help me fight the homesickness that engulfed me when I first left home and Mother was comforting to me. We slept in the same big room with several other girls, and each night she tucked me into bed and kissed me. But often my pillow was wet with tears and my heart cried out for my mother, that tender, gentle mother with the sweet smile and loving blue eyes and a touch unlike any other in the world.

Our Belstead School was a great rambling old house in the country some miles from Ipswitch. It was a remarkable school, but how old-fashioned by twentieth century standards! When my mother was a girl in the early Victorian days, the principal of this school started with a small number of young ladies whose parents were in the civil or military service in India or the colonies. In my day many of these first Belstead girls were sending their children to the same school. For instance, my mother and Lady Campbell, wife of the Governor-General of India, were at school together. The eldest Campbell daughter was at school with my sister Annie, and the younger girls were classmates with Florrie and me.

Most of the girls had the Belstead traditions before they came, so they were in harmony with the place. We were a self-governing community. Rules were made and the welfare of the community discussed in a Parliament which met every Saturday night. The older girls represented the House of Lords, the younger ones the House of Commons. We talked French one week, German the next. Our deportment was closely watched. We were drilled in calisthenics and taught to walk properly and act with dignity and restraint. Our French and German and music lessons took place in other rooms, but all our English classes were held in the big drawing room.

We drove to church in many carriages on Sunday and learned hymns on the way. We walked three and three in the narrow country lanes. Sometimes we went in the fields and by the stream to gather flowers, which we made into bouquets and sent to London hospitals. We had gala nights, when all the girls who had recently had birthdays had a table of their own and invited their special school friends to sit with them. We often studied in the lovely old garden, and we played croquet on the lawn.

When Florrie and I were together at Belstead in her second year, we were still very close. As her confidante, I knew that her friendship for Charles Barclay had grown stronger and more intimate with the passing years. They corresponded all the time. I knew that he had asked my father's permission to propose to her and that my parents had objected because she was so young. They had said, though, that after her eighteenth birthday, they would consent to an engagement if she wished it.

How far Florrie and Charles felt themselves engaged, though she was still only seventeen, even I could not determine. They saw each other often. But other young men had been attracted to Florrie, too. She had many admirers, and I used to check them off as possible or impossible. But I never thought any of them were worthy of my ideal sister, with her beautiful face and the strength and nobility of her character.

At last our school year ended. We had a happy summer together before I returned to Belstead alone. Florrie remained in Limehouse to help our mother with the parish work, but she faithfully wrote to her homesick little sister about everything that happened.

I was not nearly so homesick as I had been the year before, for I had made many friends at school. One was a bosom friend after my own heart, Birdie Anderson; she had blue eyes, fair hair and a sweet, merry smile. We had lots of fun together and, every once in a while, a bit of mischief not quite in line with the quiet decorum of the rules. The last time we met was on my wedding day, but we still feel toward each other as we did at Belstead and still correspond regularly. To me she is still "Birdie" and I "Maudie" to her, and we see each other as the laughing carefree girls of long ago.

I went home for the Christmas holiday knowing that Florrie's eventful birthday had just passed and nothing had been said. She and our mother and I went to Nutfield together, for Aunt Maria Charlesworth had died, and my mother needed to be there to supervise household matters. Then my father wrote that Charles Barclay was coming to see us.

We knew what that meant, but Florrie was surprised. My sister, always so composed and self-reliant, was filled with a restless nervousness. She told me that she did not want to be left alone. I must be with them at all times! Of course, I knew that Charles would wish me in kingdom come or anywhere out of the way. When he arrived, she would not go down to meet him unless I tagged along. We three sat around in the drawing room most inanely. I felt miserable, but if I moved, Florrie gave me a fierce look of command, and I sat down again.

Then I had a brilliant idea. Florrie was a wonderful pianist, played by the hour, and everyone enjoyed her music. I suggested that she play for us. As the three-cornered visit was a dismal failure, Charles gladly pressed her to do so. She turned to me and asked what she should play. "Beethoven's Funeral March," I said, though the imp of mischief in my mind nearly made me say "Handel's Wedding March." Florrie threw herself into her music, and I slipped quickly out of the room.

I did not know what happened when the music ceased, but there was a long, long silence. Hours afterward, I heard them calling me, and I was duly informed that they were engaged. That night Florrie told me that I need not worry or feel that I was soon to lose her. She had determined not to be married for years and years.

That was late December. On the twentieth of the following March, she and Charles Barclay were married.

I threw my soul into the preparations for the wedding. I cared far more about dresses and jewels and the pomp of ceremony than the bride-elect. She loved to dress simply, almost severely, in tailored dresses, but I was full of the glories of her trousseau. My mother and I almost had to drag her to shops and dressmakers; then she looked utterly miserable trying on silks and satins and fussing over long gloves and hat plumes.

I was more interested in the wedding itself than she was, though she was very interested, indeed, in planning with Charles Barclay about the three month honeymoon which they were to have in Palestine, a place where she had long wished to go.

Her wedding was to be the first of a Rector's daughter in our church for a hundred years or more. We knew that besides all the guests from afar, the parish people would crowd every available space. When the day came, I spread sheets on the floor to protect her satin train, then helped her to dress. She glowed in her shimmering gown with its wreath of orange blossoms, white heath and myrtle, her cloud of a veil, and her great bouquet of white orchids and lilies cut from Bury Hill greenhouses. In triumph I called up the servants so that they might gaze upon the bride.

"Lord, Miss Maudie! Don't she just look like waxworks!" exclaimed the cook, awed and admiring.

My sister gave me a look of horror, and when I had bundled all the viewers out again she exclaimed: "That settles it! As soon as you start for the church, I'll take all this stuff off and put on my little black dress with the red tie. Don't be surprised when I appear! I WON'T look like waxworks!"

I nearly cried. To comfort me, she finally promised not to rebel. After the wedding and the breakfast, when the last rice was thrown and good-byes called, my other self, my best beloved comrade, went out into the world. I slipped back to a silent house to pack an endless number of little silver boxes of wedding cake and to realize a deep empty ache in my heart.

The day after Florrie's wedding, I met the unknown man who years afterward was to become my husband. I am glad to think that my own dear mother introduced me to him. Our meeting happened in the following way.

Opposite St. Anne's Church, with its high tower, its long row of lime trees and its ancient gravestones, was a dark and dingy little theater of the lowest type called a "penny graff." When I was about twelve years of age, this place was leased and cleaned up by a little bank of workers called the Christian Mission. On Sunday afternoons they held open-air meetings at the triangle, a stone's throw from our Rectory. They sang songs, that with my church training sounded very funny to me, such as "O! You Must Be a Lover of the Lord or You Can't Go to Heaven When You Die." Then they would pray very loudly and speak even more loudly, and I, from an upstairs window, would watch a crowd gather. Often it was a very rough crowd, jostling and jeering.

The time came when the young hoodlums of the street became actively hostile, and the police stepped in and stopped the meetings, forbidding the open-air services.

My father's sense of justice brought him to the street missionaries' help. The rowdies should have been stopped and not these harmless and, he believed, sincere workers. As a rebuke to the police and to the crowd, he threw open the gates of the Rectory and allowed the Christian Mission to hold its afternoon service in our front court. This brought bigger crowds than they had ever had. A policeman watched over them; we lent them a chair for a speaker to stand on, and I sat at the window watching, listening and little knowing how my future experience would be linked with those same open-air enthusiasts.

When I was fourteen, our mother took Florrie and me to spend our summer at the seaport of Harwich, a little south of Felixstowe on the east coast. Swimming and sailing were our principal enjoyments. Because we were on the beach so much, we came into closer and more personal touch with the open-air preachers.

Our mother always associated herself with any good Christian work actively going forward in the resorts to which she took us for our holidays. While we played on the beach, she and the ladies whom she met and in whom she soon aroused an interest in Bible study, would sit in a group on the sand and have little meetings which we girls called "umbrella meetings." Our mother and her friends would sit in a ring, and to shield themselves from the sun, they would put up their umbrellas or sunshades. To us their group looked like a ring of black mushrooms. We made fun of them to ourselves, and we got a bean shooter, and I'm afraid we used it sometimes to shoot at those same umbrellas and stir the ladies up a bit. Of course, we never hurt anyone; they just wondered if some insect had struck.

Besides having her mushroom ring at Harwich, my mother became deeply interested in some of the same workers she had known as the Christian Mission, but who now called themselves the Salvation Army. The Captain and Lieutenant were two young girls, quite uneducated and with little worldly experience, but with great zeal. Much in earnest, they had reached and reformed some of the toughest sailors in the port, and these same rough men would give their testimonies in the open-air meetings.

All the town had known them as dangerous, drinking, fighting blackguards. Now they were sober, honest and hardworking, and these miracles of God's grace made a profound impression. Our mother often took us to the meetings, and we became much enthused. Once or twice we took the young girl officers out for picnics or sailing. We got to know them and admired their pluck and earnest labors. After that we ranked ourselves among the ardent defenders of the much ridiculed Salvation Army.

For the next two years, my mother kept up her interest in the Salvation Army, and every week or two went to the Friday night meeting in Whitechapel conducted by Bramwell Booth. The day after Florrie's wedding, my mother saw my loneliness and depression. She thought going to hear Bramwell Booth would cheer me. We sailed forth only to find that the leader's place had been filled in his absence by his brother Ballington.

This earnest, whole-souled young man delivered an impassioned appeal to Christians to make their Christianity a vital thing by true consecration to God's service. I was in an especially receptive mood, for I was preparing for confirmation. The thought came to me that really there was not much in me to confirm. In that meeting, for the first time, I caught sight of the vision that was to lead me to my Lord, and to make His will and His service the paramount interest in my life.

My mother introduced herself to the speaker after the meeting; then she turned to me, standing shyly behind her, and said, "Mr. Ballington Booth, this is my little daughter Maud." Little did we dream how the future would link our names together, but as I looked into those brown eyes, I thought to myself that he had eyes just like Florrie's. I believe I loved him from that moment. Bishop Walsham Howe, Bishop of Bedford, confirmed me in a solemn ceremony. The occasion was beautiful, but my heart was troubled. I was not yet sure of my spiritual life and faith. Shortly afterwards in a great meeting at Exeter Hall, an appeal was made for those who wanted to utterly and wholeheartedly consecrate their lives to God's service to rise in the audience, and I made my decision. I was very shy, very much afraid of being conspicuous. Yet my heart told me that I must make this public confession, and I thought that this was a crisis in my life. I love to remember that as I stood there, with eyes closed, praying for God's acceptance of the life I surrendered to Him, that my own beloved mother's hand clasped mine. She knelt beside me, praying for the child whose temper and willfulness and worldly-mindedness had often worried her with fears for the future.

I went back to school with a desire to study hard during my next few years to fit myself for what the future might hold. When Florrie came home from her honeymoon, she travelled to Belstead to see me and to tell me all about the new home to which she was going. Her husband was to become the Vicar of Hertford Heath, and she was full of plans for furnishing her new home. At once she entered into the parish life, which she was to make helpful and inspiring for forty years.

That summer my mother and I went to Lowestoft, a favorite summer resort of ours, and for part of the time Charles and Florrie had lodgings near us. But my blessed mother was not well. My Uncle Arthur had died, and his death had been a shock to her. I remember the day that she at last went to a doctor and how seriously she and Florrie talked together afterward. They must have known then that her life was threatened, but they kept the truth from me. Our stay was cut short by my Grandfather Beddome's death, and we hastened to his home.

At the end of the summer, I went back to school, but soon heard that Mother was far from well and was staying with my aunt at Grandfather's home. Then came the black day of fear and bewilderment when they telegraphed me to come to her at once. For three days of anguish, I sat by her side with my father and sisters, knowing each day she was slipping farther and farther from us.

When she was gone and we had laid her in that quiet Limpsfield churchyard of my babyhood memories, I felt utterly bereft. I saw Charlie put his arm around Florrie and lead her away to the carriage that would take them home. But I felt that I had no home. My mother was my home, and she was gone. The sun had gone out. I had to turn to God with the desperate weakness and loneliness that overwhelmed me.

Into that sixteenth year of my life had come two events that transformed it. One was my sister Florrie's marriage. The other was my sainted mother's death. When that year passed, I had passed from a carefree child into a woman.

Chapter 6

I GROW UP, TOO

CHILDREN TAKE ALL life's blessings for granted. All those carefree, sheltered, guarded days when someone else thinks for them and lives for them are accepted as their right and the natural process of life. Only when we look back is the deep debt of gratitude realized, and often, then, we have no chance for repayment.

At the time, I did not realize what a happy, carefree childhood I had. I did not realize how the little things that I petulantly rebelled against were laying a good foundation for the future or how the things my mother was dinning into my giddy little head would come back as guidance and inspiration later in life.

After my mother's funeral, I went back to school but never back to Limehouse, that empty home without a mother in it. My father retired from his work, and Florrie planned for me to spend my spring holiday with her. The coming of her first baby in March and all the joy we had together over that amazing, absorbing infant made life for me sweet and interesting again. I remember how lovingly Mother had bought and prepared the baby things for the little one she would never see. We had the thrill of the morning baths and dressing the tiny girl in her lovely, long robes and the christening. I almost felt that Florrie's first baby was my baby, too. Had we not always shared everything together?

But the time spent with her was only a holiday. I went back to school at Belstead and enjoyed being with Birdie Anderson and other friends again. Outside my window during that last term in school, the big fir tree had in its shady branches a concert-singing nightingale. I did not appreciate the sweetness and glory of its song then because the noise often kept me awake at night.

I did not know that I would not be returning to Belstead. My father took Annie and me to travel in the Lake Country during the summer. When they went to church, I went to Salvation Army meetings and took part in them. When autumn came, father told me we were going to Italy and to Jerusalem for the winter. He had always longed to spend time in the Holy Land and thought that he might make the Holy City his permanent home.

Our first stop was Paris. Not long after we arrived there, Catherine Booth, General William Booth's eldest daughter, came with two workers to establish the Salvation Army in France. She was the most talented of the Booth girls, a brilliant speaker and devoted worker. By that time, I had become acquainted with the second daughter, Emma, and a deep friendship had developed between us, but I did not know Catherine. My father well knew my interest in the Salvation Army, and he suggested that I call on Catherine. He had no idea what this would lead to.

Catherine Booth had begun an interesting and unique work and was carrying it on under very adverse circumstances. She was very anxious for any new helpers that she could get. Her French was neither expert nor spontaneous. Having talked French all my life, I had a gift that could help her. Learning of her problem, my father told me to go to her while he and my sister remained at their hotel. Later he added that if I really felt called to enter the work with her, I might do so. In a few days after earnest prayer on the subject, I made up my mind that the Salvation Army would be my life's work, and my father gave me his blessing.

But the night before he and Annie were to leave, I went to dine with them and a wave of homesickness overwhelmed me. I told him that I could not stay in Paris; I would leave with him. He quoted to me the Scripture that those who put their hand to the plow should not turn back. I faced the crisis and returned to my new work. My father and Annie resumed their journey. Years passed before I saw Annie again in friendly circumstances; she had become Mrs. Frederick Mann, married to a clergyman of the Church of England. My father had taken pains to give Catherine Booth twenty-five pounds to support me for the first three months, and he also gave me a French Bible inscribed with the verse he had quoted: "No man, having put his hand to the plow, and looking back, is fit for the Kingdom of God" (Luke 9:52).

There is not time or space here for me to tell of the successful work Catherine Booth did in Paris and France, or of the privations and sacrifices and difficulties. I was only an aide; Catherine was the leader and intrepid campaigner. Later we went to

Switzerland and opened the work, and a marvelous revival took place. Josephine Butler, a splendid woman who championed the cause of Europe's white slaves and was the means of rousing many people to help rescue them, was with us for awhile in Geneva. A sympathetic company of Christians rallied around us. I remember waking in our quarters at five o'clock a.m. on a Sunday morning and hearing the tramp of many feet hastening to the six-thirty a.m. meeting in the Salle de la Reformation. Two thousand people would gather there in the cold wintry dawn, while as many more would be outside unable to get in. Those meetings were really pentecostal experiences. Hundreds of converts were gathered in from among the infidel, careless, churchless masses.

One would think that Geneva, city of early Reformation fame, would have rejoiced at such scenes. Alas! The fair city was in the hands of a very corrupt political ring. The Chief of Police was hand in glove with the saloons and white slave traffic. The people, whose poor victims were wrested from them and whose traffic was fearlessly attacked, became very bitter against the little band of Salvationists. The whole affair is documented history and was presented to the British Parliament in a Blue Book. The hoodlums were incited to stone and mob us; the police were instructed to arrest us for being mobbed and attacked, so that we might be suppressed as disturbers of the peace.

Apart from my joy at the glorious work being accomplished, I was also thrilled by the excitement of the police persecution. We discovered that we were being shadowed everywhere by detectives. The police raked up an old law that had not been enforced for a hundred years, having then been used against the Jesuits. The law stated in effect, that no public meetings of a religious order could be convened without permits from the police.

The police refused to give us the permits, thus closing the Salle de la Reformation to us. But we had with us as strong supporters some of the finest people of Geneva: bankers, ministers, ladies of wealth and title and the college students. They opened their drawing rooms for our meetings. Our humbler converts opened their kitchens or even their attic rooms. Instead of putting out the fire of revival, the police scattered it all over the city.

Since our forces had to separate for the many small meetings, I was often the leader of one of them, and I began to speak in public. My father and his forefathers for generations had been preachers. My mother was an easy and appealing speaker. Words seemed to come naturally to me, and in Geneva, where French predominated, I had the advantage of thinking and speaking in French as well as English.

I had a background of pure English language and an ancestry of the best legal minds as a Charlesworth. I was only seventeen in those Geneva days, and I was shy and diffident when I started, but after my first public talk, I faced the problem of "stage fright" and fought it out. I concluded that the fear came from self-consciousness and from the dread of appearing foolish or saying the wrong thing. This fear might be justified if I were lecturing on theories of my own, or going in for dramatic art, recitations, or anything secular. But if I was delivering God's message to the hearts of men, I was only a messenger. I must absolutely forget myself and pass on to others what was given me to say.

From that time I was never nervous or afraid. Of course, I had much to learn and have been learning all my life about ways to deal with a crowd, how to make illustrations carry home the truth, and how to use the proper method of delivery and the carrying power of the voice. But I have always kept the inspiring thought: I am trying to give God's message; He can inspire and direct and guide my mind and heart, and His words shall not fall to the ground unheeded.

The good work went on in Geneva and despite, or maybe because of, persecution became the talk of Switzerland and, later, the talk of Europe. The police made a very bad move which caused the people of religious tolerance to rise to defend us.

The police had determined to arrest and expel La Marechale, her chief of staff and her little aide-de-camp. I was the first to go.

We were to have a gathering of our converts at an old farm two miles out of the city. La Marechale was at a drawing room group meeting in town. I went with about a hundred of our soldiers, all supposed to be invited guests. While we were at prayer, two men dressed as peasants and looking just like the other folk who had come into the house entered and worshiped with us. They were police spies, and since we did not stop our prayer to challenge them, they reported that we had had a public gathering violating the law.

The next morning before we were up, two big, formidable police officers were at the door of our quarters with a warrant for my arrest. I had to dress hurriedly and go with them, and they allowed me no breakfast. We must have looked foolish, even to the passersby: a short, slim, slip of a girl of seventeen, who could not look like a criminal by any stretch of the imagination, being marshalled through the streets by those husky officers of the law. At their office, they gave me a third-degree examination that lasted from early morning until late at night, with no food for me and not one of our friends or fellow-workers allowed to come near me.

Fortunately, I have always had a sense of humor, and I also had a thorough command of their language. I did not lose my self-control, and I did not allow them to frighten me. Their idea was to question me and from my answers manufacture facts enabling them to expel us all. When they got weary late at night, they demanded my signature to the documents purporting to be my declaration. I utterly refused to sign anything unless one of our lawyer friends read and approved it. At last, they gave up, and I had the joy of seeing a friendly face waiting for me. I was allowed to go.

La Marechale had been moved to a friend's house, and I was taken, exhausted but triumphant, to join her. Surely they could do no more.

But they did. Just after breakfast the next morning, a carriage arrived with three police officers. In the presence of our indignant friends, my order of expulsion was read to us.

I only had time to pack a handbag, and then with my police escort, I was driven off to some unmentioned point across the border in France. I shed no tears. My fighting blood was up. Crowds in the street waved goodbye and jeered at the police. On the road outside the city, a group of our dear people sang hymns and waved to me as I passed. The spirit of one of my Hugenot ancestors whispered encouragement, so I really enjoyed that drive tremendously.

At last, we passed out of the canton, over a stream and away from the jurisdiction of the authorities. The police, having driven me so far against my will, might have been kind enough to take me a little farther to a hotel. But no! They were too mad at the whole situation. They dumped me by the roadside, turned their horses and galloped back to Geneva. I picked up my little bag and trudged in the other direction, not knowing where I was. Luckily, a clean, little hotel was not far away. There, after telegraphing in code to my friends in Geneva, I took up my abode. I did not have long to wait. Two days later La Marechale was expelled. Then we waited together, and Colonel Arthur Clibborn arrived, also dealt with by the law.

By this time the newspapers of Europe were full of our expulsion, though we did not realize it. Out to our little hotel came a London *Times* reporter. He wanted all the details for his paper. After Colonel Clibborn and Miss Booth had talked to him, he asked me for an account of my experiences.

During my two days of lonely exile, I wrote an account, including a rather intimately funny description of the police examination, to General William Booth in London. It was meant just as a personal letter. As it had not been mailed, La Marechale told our friend of the *Times* to look it through and then to mail it for us.

My first encounter with a reporter cost me years of bitter experience. He took the letter and printed it in full in the *Times* with the title "Lamb Among Wolves." The unknown little seventeen-year-old Maud Charlesworth became notorious. I was aghast when a telegram came from my father ordering me home. I was overwhelmed when I read the papers and found myself public property. I had been brought up to think that anything of that sort was practically a disgrace. People accustomed to personal publicity in the press today can hardly understand how I felt. I wept in shame over "Lamb Among Wolves," though the newspaper comments were friendly, even almost fatherly.

The English ambassador was ordered to see us and remonstrate about our treatment. The world stood by us, and the police were violently censured. But I had to suffer personally for years, and even at that time I felt as if my privacy had been violated. My father's church friends blamed him for leaving me "unprotected in Switzerland." They inveighed against the Salvation Army. There I was with an angry parent shocked and surprised at me and demanding that I leave the work I loved and had given my life to.

I looked at the French Bible in which my father had written the verse about "hand to the plough," and I wrote him that my lot was cast with the Salvation Army and I could not turn back.

These experiences brought about a long and sad separation and a breaking of old family ties. That bitter newspaper controversy ostracized me except from Florrie, who never deserted me. The next time I visited my father's home, he called the servants up as I left as witnesses that I was never to return. My few possessions were packed and sent after me. As far as my father was concerned, I was also to be disinherited.

In France and Switzerland, led and molded by the influence of La Marechale Catherine Booth and Arthur Clibborn, the Salvation Army movement was a beautiful one, simple and apostolic-like, a gathering together of self-sacrificing and spiritual souls. People have been accustomed to speak of General William Booth as having made the Salvation Army. He was indeed its founder, and he was a great genius in many ways. But his wife Catherine Booth was a great spiritual power behind him. She was one of the most devoted, most outstanding women of the Nineteenth Century. I can say from long years of personal knowledge that General Booth's children, especially Bramwell, but Ballington, La Marechale Catherine, Emma and Herbert, too, were the ones who built and organized and energized the Salvation Army into international influence. They were all greatly inspired by their mother as well as their father. Because of them Salvationism was, in considerable part at least, an enthusiastic youth movement.

Chapter 7

DIFFICULT ENGAGEMENT, HAPPY ENDING

AFTER A THRILLING year in Switzerland and France, and staying with the Booth family in England on various occasions, a glorious thing had come into my life, the greatest gift after God's love and His call to service. I was back in Paris, France, with Catherine when Ballington Booth visited us. In a lovely park as we walked and talked together, he asked me to be his wife. I was very young, but I felt myself a grown woman. Ballington was my ideal, my knight of romance. But even then we both felt that we must put the work first and could only be married if we were sure that we could help each other to greater service.

On Ballington's return to London, his father, at

my father's request, forbade any acknowledged engagement until I was eighteen. After that birthday, I went back to England usually staying with the Booth family, but his father kept Ballington travelling. At last, however, I put on the Salvation Army uniform which my father had forbidden me to wear until that age. Back at home, Ballington went to see Reverend Charlesworth to ask his permission for our marriage.

My father received him graciously enough, but told him plainly that he would never consent. He had nothing against my beloved; he would accept him and send him to college if he would leave the Salvation Army and enter the Church of England. But he did not want his daughter to marry into the Salvation Army. After I had gone myself to see him and my firm resolve to marry Ballington was made clear, he disinherited me.

So Ballington and I faced the fact that we could not marry until I reached the age of twenty-one. His father sent him to help build the Salvation Army work in Australia, and we could enjoy our engagement only through lengthy letters, six weeks old when they reached us.

My assignment was to travel through England and Ireland, Scotland and Wales, holding services and gathering funds for the maintenance of the officers' training home. I had become so well known publicly through the excitement in Switzerland and my father's denunciation of the Salvation Army that my name drew crowds wherever I was to speak.

Ballington had founded and built up the work of training the future officers of the movement. Most of those who became the ablest and most useful all over the world were once his training home boys and owed everything to his earnest inspiration. So in my loneliness during his absence, my joy was to gather funds to carry on the work now under his brother Herbert. I raised hundreds of pounds for the training home and also helped many of the local posts and divisions.

If there was any town in special need of help, I would be sent there for some days to raise friends and meet with the converts and then help Headquarters visualize the difficulties. Often, as a clergyman's daughter, and one with past good connections, I would be accorded entrance to those who had prejudice against the local workers.

Then came an experience that I shall always look back to as one of vital influence in all my afterwork. The Salvation Army was working among the poor, the ignorant, the unchurched, but reaching mostly the working class. In London there was a class far lower still which even the Army's ordinary street meetings and open-air work could not reach. These people were the denizens of unspeakable slums, people existing in squalor and filth and degradation, bitter against the world, a prey to misfortune and vice and often sodden with drink.

Emma Booth and I talked over the problem of reaching and helping these people when we were at the training home. We hit on the idea of exploring the situation by going in disguise to live among the dwellers in slumdom. I was commissioned for the work with three other young women. One was Blanche Cox; the other names I forget. We gathered some old, disreputable furniture, dressed in the poorest of clothing with shawls over our heads instead of hats and established the first slum center. We were the pioneers of much later slum work, but our efforts are long forgotten. We lived among poor match workers, washed little babies for their weary mothers, scrubbed countless floors and tried to preach simple sermons of loving service as we did our best to enact them. But that experience was only one of the smaller stones built into the house of memory that has been my life.

Between my travels and my slum work and all

sorts of happy, busy days, I lived with Mrs. General Booth. We were very close together in heart. To know that this devoted mother, this great preacher and altogether consecrated woman loved me as a daughter was a joy. She wholeheartedly rejoiced with me in my love for her son and my intended union with him. We talked together a great deal, and she gave me wise and common sense advice on my Christian life that counterbalanced the natural emotionalism of youth. My relations with my future brothers and sisters-in-law were happy, and my position in the work was one of usefulness and constant activity.

At that time the Salvation Army was being much annoyed by bands of rowdies and hoodlums who called themselves the "Skeleton Army". They marched alongside our people, throwing stones and pushing and jostling them. Their yells and threats broke up street meetings. Because of their riotousness, authorities in some towns suppressed open-air work altogether.

One seaside town was the worst, and I was commissioned to go down there for a week or two and fight it out. It was an interesting experience. I got the "Skeletons" together and talked to them of my experience in Switzerland. I asked them to form my bodyguard, for we feared the police were against us. We thought that some element we could not see was back of all the trouble, and we wanted to enlist their help. We would welcome the "Skeletons", but they must march in front of us and behind us when we marched and be our protectors. I had special meetings for the "Skeletons" only, and treated them as our friends and allies. They agreed to an armistice, and we had a most joyous time together. The treaty of peace lasted until the cause of it had been forgotten and tolerance reigned.

My last outstanding experience before my marriage was my visit to Sweden and my meetings with the students of Uppsala. In the summer of 1885, Catherine Booth, La Marechale, and I were both exhausted to the point of illness. Mrs. General Booth, the older Catherine, thought that we were not really intellectually prepared for our religious work and should study theology. So we were sent back to Switzerland, not to work but to rest. Three hours in the morning and three hours in the afternoon we concentrated on theological learning. I never tried very hard to remember much of it. The people I have dealt with all my life have needed the two great commandments, and the knowledge that somebody loves and cares for them, more than they have ever needed any of the intellectual arguments of theology.

Being well and back into active work felt good. I had passed my twentieth birthday and was looking forward to the events of the year which, on my coming of age, would leave me free to marry. My beloved was doing fine Army work in Australia. The long, long letters that crossed the many years dividing us were making us better and better acquainted with each other's thoughts and ambitions, joys and sorrows, ideals and aspirations; but separation was hard for us. I just tried to fill my days with work and to believe that every day was better fitting me to be my wonderful lover's wife. The responsibilities of wifehood and comradeship loomed up before me as tremendous, especially with Mrs. General Booth's counsel and advice on the subject.

My commission in Sweden was a responsible one. I was to represent Headquarters to review the country. Work had been going on there for four years but with little enthusiastic acceptance and some opposition.

I took a secretary with me, and we had a terribly rough voyage, landing with great relief in the beautiful land of pine forests and blue lakes and glorious starlight and moonlight nights.

I loved the country and grew very fond of its people, and my journeys took me as far as Sundvale in the north. There was a devoted leader in charge in Sweden and many able workers. The companies of converts whom I met were enthusiastic, even if the general population was not.

Going home late one night from a public meeting in the town of Uppsala, I found the street made noisy by a band of students, all boisterously drunk. My group stopped and looked into the saloons and found them crowded by these young university men, the very flower of Sweden. Down some of the shadier streets, we saw groups of them gathered with those who could only contaminate them and ruin their future.

"What are we doing for the students?" I asked. The answer was "nothing."

Two students had become interested in the Salvation Army, and one was now a prominent officer, but no special effort had been made to reach this big body of youth, so full of life and energy and talent.

In my room that night, I prayed for the students and thought about them for a long time. I was still only a girl, but because of my work I often felt old in experience. Still, to reach and influence this great student body did seem impossible. The more I thought, however, I felt that God had laid upon my heart the need to do something.

I talked to the Swedish leader of the work, and with the two students, we evolved an idea. Why not announce a meeting for students only, when I could talk to them, using my name and Swiss experience as a drawing card.

"You can invite them, but they won't come," others told us. "Or if they do come, they will make a riot of it. Students rule in this city, and they do very much as they please."

After a little more thought, we hit on the idea of placarding the city with big posters in Latin, announcing that students only were invited to meet the Miss Charlesworth of Switzerland, and that no one not a member of their body would be admitted. One night we literally painted the town red with our proclamation. The next morning all over the city, groups of students were reading the signs and talking about the meeting. Until the appointed hour came, we had no way of knowing how they would respond.

Yes, we got the crowd! I knew that, as I sat in the little back room waiting for the hour of meeting. I heard the steady tramp, tramp, tramp of feet.

Someone came to tell me that every seat was taken and all the standing room filled. Presently, I heard the rap, tap of countless canes calling me out. As never before, I realized my smallness and insufficiency for the great message in my heart. I knelt alone and prayed for God's guidance.

Here I was, a girl of twenty, undertaking to guide and teach this vast assembly of young university men. What would they do? Laugh at me? Get up and leave the hall when I began to speak? Play tricks to break up the gathering? Perhaps I should have listened to older heads and refrained from the attempt.

Then, as never before in my life, came the thought that I was only a messenger. These boys were the future leaders of Sweden, but many of them were godless, throwing away their chances, soiling their young manhood. If God had something to say to them, He could say it through my lips, however weak and trembling. The result was in His divine hands. So as I knelt and prayed, all fear left me. Joyously, I stepped out onto the platform with my heart throbbing with new inspiration.

What an audience! Just a sea of smiling, questioning faces, and a long deep silence. One of our student officers spoke a word of earnest prayer. Then came my chance. I spoke no Swedish, but I had a splendid rapid interpreter, so that I did not feel the handicap of language. For two hours and more, I passed on the message that came to me. Every now and then a ripple of response passed over the audience, but for the most part there was an intense silence, then unlooked for tears. I saw some heads bowed and some boys quietly wiping their eyes. Others, absolutely oblivious to the fellows next to them, let the tears flow unhidden.

I felt like an onlooker watching the response of human hearts to God's touch, God's call and appeal. As I sat down there was silence—a long, dead silence. Then came such acclaim as I have rarely heard: applause, shouts and calls for me to come again. Their hearts were mine.

After that night I was called in the Swedish papers "Miss Charlesworth of Uppsala." The students claimed me. They came to my meetings en masse. Numbers stayed for the intimate prayer meeting after our public meetings and sought Christ as their Savior. Some who were infidels yielded to God's revelation. Others who had been hard drinkers and were leading fast lives showed by their absolute change of conduct the sincerity of their change of heart. I did not really know all of this, however, until letters began pouring in from their mothers in homes all over Sweden showing me how understandingly these boys had accepted my message. The mothers wrote thanking me for my influence over their dear ones, and I smiled as I read, wondering what those dear mothers would say if they could see how very young and inexperienced was the one to whom they wrote.

One mother told me that her son had related that the boys had gone to my meeting in the spirit of fun, armed with whistles and canes to whistle and thump me down at a given signal, but that they forgot all about their plan when I spoke.

The whole affair made quite a stir in the press, especially when a large part of the student body came below the windows of the place where I stayed and serenaded me one moonlight night. The choral society of Uppsala University was known throughout Europe for their wonderful singing, but the students had never been known before to go *en masse* to serenade anyone but the royal family of Sweden.

I remember that night so well as I sat with my friends at the lighted window and listened to the glorious voices. How thoughtfully they chose the themes—not silly love songs, but splendid inspirational words. I looked down on the upturned faces and silently prayed that their enthusiasm might live long after the memory of my face and voice had faded. When the singing stopped, one who had been chosen by his fellows stepped close and offered me the Chaplaincy of the University. If I would stay and preach to them, they swore that they would all attend the services and be my devoted followers. The student poet laureate wrote a poem to me which I kept, and I was given a button and ribbon to wear, with the colors of Uppsala. I could tell them only that I must go on to Stockholm and would try to return for another meeting. I knew what they did not, that all their enthusiastic invitations could not keep me, for even then on the other side of the world the one heart that held my destiny was planning to return and claim me.

Afterward many people, not realizing how truly a sincere spiritual message can raise a friendship above a foolishly sentimental attitude, laughingly asked me how many students had proposed to me. Years afterward, the Swedish Ambassador to Washington asked that my husband and I might be invited to a dinner given in his honor. We talked of those Uppsala days, and he said smilingly to the company, "Every student at Uppsala was in love with her." But one of my special joys at the time was that I received no silly letters, not one foolish proposal and, with all those young men around me, never a flirtatious look or action.

In Stockholm I became quite sick with a fever which lasted ten days. The time of my departure for England drew near, and I doubted that my doctor would allow me to return to Uppsala for a farewell meeting. Each day some student came to learn how I progressed, and to bring me flowers. Then they announced at the University that, if I were allowed to return, a flag would be raised on the building to announce my coming. I was told that groups of students stood around that day anxiously watching, and when the flag went up, the news ran through the college like wildfire. The professors gave up their lectures and a holiday was proclaimed. On my arrival the hall was packed to capacity.

We had a happy goodbye gathering. When the meeting was over, I had to hurry to my train. On leaving the building, still in great good spirits because the students had seemed so friendly and full of enthusiasm, I was disappointed to find the streets empty. Not a student was in sight to wave goodbye to me. On reaching the depot, however, the reason was plain. They had taken the place by storm. I walked through a narrow lane flanked by a mass of white-capped students. Boarding the train, my secretary and I opened the windows to look over the mass of eager, smiling faces. A tiny boy was lifted to the window to present me with a glorious bunch of white roses tied with yellow and blue ribbons, the University colors. He was like a little cherub with his golden curls and blue eyes and flushed baby cheeks. No human mind could have foretold that he would meet me again twenty years later in a prison cell in Sing Sing.

There was a last ringing shout and, as the train started, a student song of farewell. I carried away an unfading picture that lives with me still, although I have never revisited Sweden. Years after in different parts of this dear land of ours, the United States, I have heard echoes of those Uppsala days. I wonder if some of the Swedish students remember. They must all be whitehaired by now, fathers and grandfathers, yet sometimes golden memories of our young days retain their colors more vividly than later happenings.

The boat from Sweden reached England two or three days before my beloved's boat arrived from Australia. Though I was engrossed in a serious service in life, I had all the heart throbs and thrills and questions of any other twenty-year-old sweetheart. Would he love me as I hoped? Would he find me improved? Was I more suitable to be his wife than when we last met? I never had a doubt that he was my beau ideal, my one gloriously perfect man, but would I be equal to the great privilege and responsibility of being his wife?

Our engagement was a very serious thing to us, because in one sense our work, God's work, must come first in our lives. I knew that had Ballington ever become convinced that I was not the one who could help him to greater service and fill the position of a co-leader in it, he would break our engagement and cut me out of his heart. His whole training and upbringing had been "first the Kingdom," and two years had passed since we had seen each other.

In May of 1886, we had a happy reunion. Still, we could not marry until my twenty-first birthday and kept busy with the Salvation Army's first International Congress and with international groups touring Britain for a month afterward. But at last my longed for birthday came.

We were married three days later, September 16, in the Salvation Army's big Congress Hall in London. General William Booth performed the ceremony before a crowd of five thousand. My father refused to come, but my beloved Florrie came, and her husband Charles Barclay, my brother-in-law, took me on his arm and gave me away. I wore no white dress with veil and orange blossoms, but a plain blue uniform with a white scarf draped across the shoulder. The only relief to the severity of my clothing was a spray of white roses and myrtle. But I was supremely happy.

That was the beginning of a long married life in which our love deepened and strengthened and widened. Looking back on all we have shared, I think we know what marriage was meant to be, and how absolutely and wonderfully it can enhance and glorify life.

EPILOGUE

MAUD AND BALLINGTON Booth began making American friends on the ship which brought them and a few British Salvationists to New York harbor on April 18, 1887. Their assignment was to unite and supervise the competing small groups of English immigrants who had brought loyalty to their Army with them. The new leaders' friendliness made that easy, and they made more friends and converts each year, organizing them in military ranks, like the British Salvation Army. Supreme authority stayed with General William Booth in England; Commander Ballington represented him in the United States. Ballington was an expert organizer; Maud developed women's auxiliaries, and together their groups, however poor themselves, worked to help the poor in their communities. The "posts" of the American Salvation Army spread widely. Ballington and Maud made several trips to England to make sure their work was approved.

In their eighth year in the United States, 1894, General William Booth came to inspect their troops. Maud and Ballington arranged welcoming ceremonies in many posts so that he could visit from New York west to Chicago. He was impressed by the size of the crowds and their enthusiasm, but he resented their proud slogan "For God and Country," when so obviously their displays of the United States flag, and banners with the American eagle showed that their country was America. The Booths then needed a new Chief Secretary, but General William forbade them to appoint the American one they wanted, and sent over a British officer whom he personally chose. The Secretary was officious and critical, and sometimes gave orders contrary to those of Ballington. Ballington eventually asked for the Secretary's recall, but his father refused. General Booth had always preached "adaptability", but would not hear Ballington's explanations of why his work in the United States required it. In a final disagreement, William Booth in 1896 dismissed Ballington and Maud from the leadership of the Salvation Army in the United States and ordered them to report immediately to England.

They made no public protest, but they did not go. Announcement of their dismissal roused dismay and rebellion in the America ranks. New York newspapers blasted the Booths' British critics. Ballington and Maud accepted the dismissal as quietly as possible; but they were a bit desperate. They were ordered to leave their little house, owned by the Salvation Army, immediately. Their joint salary had been only $18 a week; they had no savings, and they had two small children to care for. A staunch supporter hid them at his home until he could buy back their tiny home for them. When Reverend Charlesworth in England, reconciled with his daughter on an earlier visit to the United States, heard of their plight, he promptly sent money to help them survive. Friends and supporters, who bitterly resented their treatment, urged them to start a new religious charitable organization. With many Salvation Army personnel ready to follow them, a constitution was drawn up and the formation of a new organization made public at a rousing meeting at New York's Cooper Union on March 8, 1896. Their democratic constitution, even though they kept the military set-up they were used to, showed plainly, by contrast, what had chiefly caused their trouble. Parts read:

"All properties, real estate or personal, of the Volunteers of America shall be held by a body or board composed of five to seven well-known and responsible American citizens...

"In the Volunteers, property will be held by Trustees chosen for the purpose, instead of being deeded over to one man...

"The Volunteers of America is, and ever must be, an American institution, recognizing the spirit and practice of the Constitution of the United States; and it is not, and never shall be, controlled or governed by any foreign power whatsoever."

In short, every local post would choose its own representatives of its military ranks to the Grand Field Council, which in turn elected the National Commander. Democracy replaced authoritarianism. Women were to rank equally with men—in that, at least the Salvation Army had pioneered.

Ballington Booth was promptly elected General or President, Maud as Vice President. The rest of the Booth family denounced them as traitors. But many outraged Salvationists, high and low, resigned from the Salvation Army and went to work for the new and untried organization, risking their livelihoods.

Ballington and Maud worked furiously with their old troops to win new ones. In six months they established 140 posts with 400 commanding officers, 50 staff officers, three regiments and 10 battalions. From their first rented "Office" in the Bible House—a single room furnished with orange crates and packing box furniture, they were soon able to spread into three rooms, then into a whole floor. When they were able to buy a small building with three floors for their Headquarters, the Volunteers of America felt assured that they had a future.

Ironically, General William Booth learned slowly, but he learned. To his other children who controlled the American Salvation Army after Ballington and Maud had been forced out, he granted most of the changes in policy that Maud and Ballington had asked for. But the names of Maud and Ballington Booth were officially erased from Salvation Army history.

—*Susan F. Welty*